100 facts

Birds of

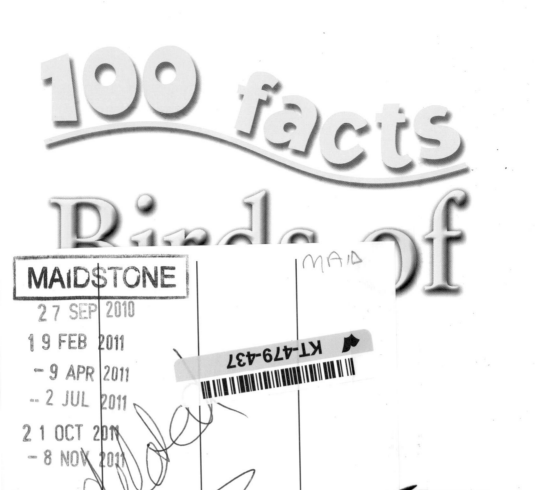

100 facts

Birds of Prey

Camilla de la Bedoyere

Consultant: Steve Parker

Miles Kelly

First published in 2010 by Miles Kelly Publishing Ltd
Bardfield Centre, Great Bardfield, Essex, CM7 4SL, UK

2 4 6 8 10 9 7 5 3 1

Editorial Director: Belinda Gallagher
Art Director: Jo Brewer
Editor: Sarah Parkin
Volume Designer: Joe Jones
Image Manager: Liberty Newton
Indexer: Jane Parker
Production Manager: Elizabeth Brunwin
Reprographics: Stephan Davis, Ian Paulyn

ISBN 978-1-84810-263-7

Printed in China

British Library Cataloguing-in-Publication Data
A catalogue record for this book is available from the British Library

ACKNOWLEDGEMENTS
The publishers would like to thank the following artists
who have contributed to this book:
Mike Foster (Maltings Partnership), Ian Jackson,
Barry Jones, Mike Saunders
All other artworks are from the Miles Kelly Artwork Bank

The publishers would like to thank the following sources
for the use of their photographs:
t = top, b = bottom, l = left, r = right
Cover Jeremy Woodhouse/Getty Images
Pages 2–3 Markus Varesvuo/naturepl.com; 6–7 Wild Wonders of Europe/Nill/naturepl.com; 10(t) Igor Shpilenok/naturepl.com,
(br) Andy Rouse/Photoshot; 11(t) Tony Heald/naturepl.com, (br) John Cancalosi/naturepl.com; 15 Markus Varesvuo/naturepl.com;
16 Juan Carlos Munoz/naturepl.com; 18 Shawn P. Carey (Migration Productions); 19 Laurie Goodrich, Hawk Mountain Sanctuary, USA;
20–21 A & J Visage/Alamy; 22 javarman/Fotolia.com; 23 Jordi Bas Casas/Photoshot; 24–25 Markus Varesvuo/naturepl.com;
24(bl) Arthur Morris/Corbis; 27 Luis Quinta/naturepl.com; 29 Imagebroker, Bernd Zoller, Image/FLPA;
30 Jordi Bas Casas/Photoshot; 31 blickwinkel/Alamy; 33 Ramon Navarro/Minden Pictures/FLPA;
34–35 W. Perry Conway/Corbis; 37 Roger Tidman/FLPA; 39 Sandor H.Szabo/epa/Corbis; 42(t) Peter Arnold, Inc./Alamy,
(b) David Norton/rspb-images.com; 44 Ralph Clevenger/Corbis; 45(t) Frans Lanting/FLPA; 46 John Cancalosi/naturepl.com;
47(t) M. Watson/Ardea, (b) Mark Newman/FLPA

All other photographs are from:
digitalSTOCK, digitalvision

Made with paper from a sustainable forest

www.mileskelly.net
info@mileskelly.net

www.factsforprojects.com
The one-stop homework helper – pictures, facts, videos, projects and more

www.raptorfoundation.org.uk

The publishers would like to thank The Raptor
Foundation for their help in compiling this book.

Contents

Hunters of the sky

1 Birds of prey are magnificent hunters of the sky. They soar through the air using their large wings to keep them aloft, as they scan the ground below for food. Some birds of prey, such as eagles, are hunters and kill to eat. Others, such as vultures, eat carrion (dead animals). Birds of prey are also called raptors, from the Latin *rapere*, meaning to grab or seize, because they kill with their feet.

▼ A long-legged buzzard brings food to its chicks. These birds of prey nest on cliff ledges and feed on small mammals, reptiles and large insects.

Eagle-eyed predators

2 Like all hunters, birds of prey need to be kitted out with tools. They have sharp senses, muscular bodies, tough beaks and grasping feet with sharp talons. They can detect prey from great distances and launch deadly attacks with skill and accuracy. Some can fly at super speeds.

▼ Golden eagles are large birds, measuring about 2 metres from wing tip to wing tip.

Finger-like primary flight feathers at wing tips

Rusty brown feathers

3 Raptors are able to fly high above the ground. The sky not only offers a great view of prey, it is also a safe place for birds as they search. As adults, birds of prey do have natural enemies, but even on land they are usually a match for most other predators due to their size.

4 Good eyesight is essential for raptors. They need to be able to locate prey that is in grass or under cover, often from a great distance. Birds of prey have eyes that are packed with light-detecting cells. The eyes are positioned near the front of the head, which means a bird can see well in front, to the side and partly around to the back.

▼ Birds of prey have large eyes that face forwards, to give them excellent vision.

The area of binocular vision

Peripheral vision

There is only a small 'blind area' behind the bird

QUIZ

Which of these animals are predators and which are prey?
Leopard Warthog
Eagle Crocodile
Tortoise Wildebeest

Answers:
Predators: leopard, eagle, crocodile
Prey: warthog, tortoise, wildebeest

5 **Birds of prey have big, powerful bodies.** This helps them catch and kill food, but means they need more energy to fly. Meat is an energy-packed food, ideal for building muscles. Even the largest birds of prey can swoop and soar, although smaller birds are usually more acrobatic in flight.

Pale feathers on crown

Large, broad wings

▶ Eagles and vultures have big, tough bills, but falcons have smaller, sharp bills. A bird's bill and talons are made of a hard substance called keratin, the same as our nails.

Large bill

Large tail

Powerful feet with sharp talons

Birds of prey may carry their food to a safe place to eat it, but others eat their prey where it was killed

White-tailed eagle
Large, heavy bill

Egyptian vulture
Long, hooked bill

Gyrfalcon
Short bill with a sharp hook

6 **Scientists used to think that all birds of prey had a poor sense of smell.** The turkey vulture is the only bird of prey known to have a good sense of smell, and probably the only one able to smell out its food. They can detect carrion on the ground while they are flying.

Where in the world?

▲ Steller's sea eagle eats mainly fish, so this bird of prey lives near rivers, lakes and seashores. It only breeds in far eastern Russia.

7 **Warm, tropical regions are home to many species (types) of birds of prey.** They live on grasslands or in rainforests where there is lots to eat. Away from the tropics there are fewer raptors. Their habitats include forests, wetlands and coastal areas.

▼ Peregrine falcons are one of the world's most common birds of prey and they live on every continent, except Antarctica.

8 **Birds of prey live all over the world, except Antarctica.** No raptors can survive the freezing conditions of the south polar region, where food is scarce. Some are able to find food and endure the cold of the northern Arctic area. Snowy owls, peregrine falcons and white-tailed eagles can all cope with the cold, but travel to warmer places when the worst weather bites.

▶ Vultures and a jackal fight over the carcass of a zebra on an African grassland.

9 **Some birds of prey can live in different habitats in different parts of the world.** Ospreys and peregrine falcons are found in the Americas, Africa, Asia, Europe and Australia. Ospreys prefer to live near water, while peregrines like hills, cliffs and even cities.

▶ This family of Harris hawks has made a prickly home out of a cactus. In deserts, trees are scarce.

10 **Barn owls live in many parts of the world, but one of their favourite places to build a nest is inside an old building.** They frequently choose barns or church steeples to live in, where they are unlikely to be disturbed and can find a good supply of small rodents to eat.

11 **Harris hawks hunt in deserts and other dry places.** Small animals that live in these places often stay hidden from view and out of the strong sunlight, which makes them hard to find. Smart Harris hawks deal with this problem by living and hunting in groups, which makes it easier for them to seek and kill their fast-moving prey.

Little and large

12 **The largest birds of prey are Andean condors.** Their wingspan, which is measured from wing tip to wing tip, can be 3 metres in males. Condors have the biggest wings of all birds, which can catch the wind to soar above mountains at incredible heights of 5.5 kilometres.

Andean condor
Body length: 120 centimetres
Average wingspan: 3 metres

▶ These wings are shown to scale. Large birds with big wings are able to soar and travel long distances. Birds with smaller wings are more agile in flight and can hunt at greater speeds.

Black-thighed falconet
ACTUAL SIZE

13 **In Europe, the largest raptors are white-tailed eagles.** They are found from Greenland to Turkey, but there are just 10,000 in the wild. These birds came close to extinction after years of shooting and poisoning, but are now protected in many countries. In Australia, the largest raptors are wedge-tailed eagles. They can grow to more than one metre long, with a wingspan of up to 2.3 metres.

◀ Little black-thighed falconets can easily dart through forests to hunt prey because of their small size.

14 **The smallest birds of prey are the falconets from Southeast Asia.** There are five species and the smallest are the white-fronted falconet and the black-thighed falconet. Falconets are just 14 to 18 centimetres long from bill to tail tip. Most feed on insects, but the pied falconet, which is the largest, can catch small animals.

MEASURING SIZE

Using a measuring tape, discover just how large or small these birds are. If you were standing next to an Eurasian eagle owl, would it reach your waist? If your arms were wings, what would your wingspan measure?

Eurasian eagle owl
Body length: 70 centimetres
Average wingspan: 2 metres

15 **Some owls are big birds.** Eurasian eagle owls are about 70 centimetres tall and they are large enough to hunt deer fawns, although they also eat beetles, rats and voles. They can hunt in forests, but they prefer open spaces.

Common buzzard
Body length: 48 centimetres
Average wingspan: 125 centimetres

16 **The largest bird of prey that ever lived was probably Haast's eagle.** It lived in New Zealand until around 500 years ago. Six million years ago, a giant bird called *Argentavis* flew across what is now Argentina. It had a body like a condor, but its wingspan was similar to that of a small plane!

Black-thighed falconet
Body length: 15 centimetres
Average wingspan:
30 centimetres

Hovering and soaring

17 Birds of prey have one advantage over most other predators – they can fly. Flying allows creatures to escape from other animals and stay safe. They can explore new areas easily as they search for food, mates or places to breed.

18 Birds' bodies are perfectly adapted for flying. They have light bones that are mostly hollow, but still strong. Their big hearts and lungs can collect lots of oxygen with every breath. This is the gas that animals need to turn their food into energy.

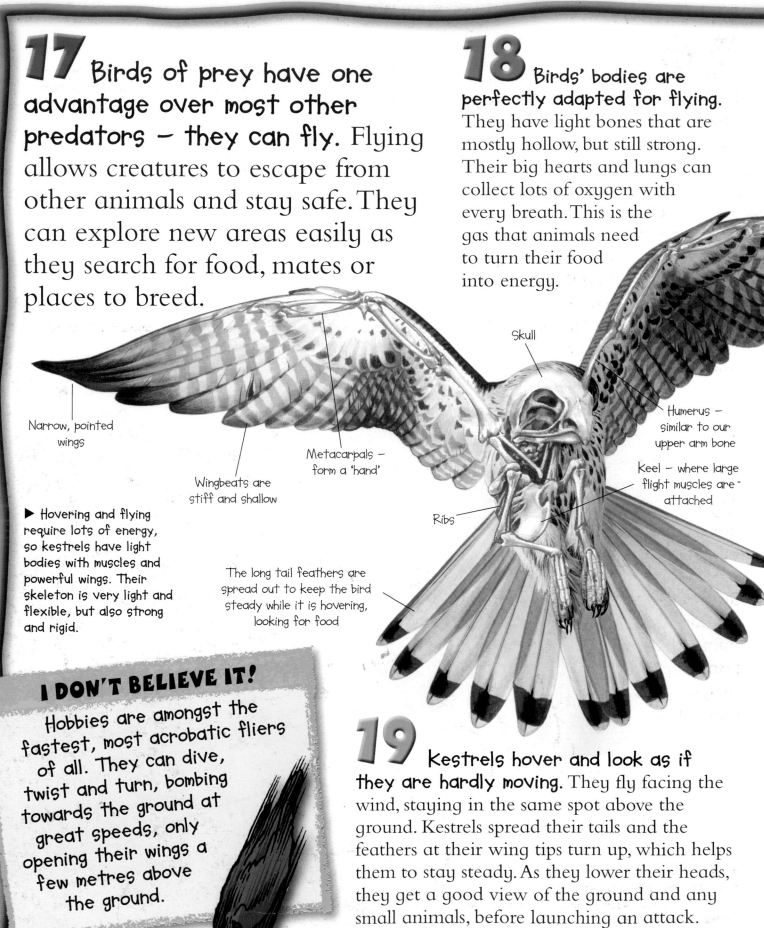

Narrow, pointed wings

Wingbeats are stiff and shallow

Metacarpals – form a 'hand'

Skull

Humerus – similar to our upper arm bone

Keel – where large flight muscles are attached

Ribs

▶ Hovering and flying require lots of energy, so kestrels have light bodies with muscles and powerful wings. Their skeleton is very light and flexible, but also strong and rigid.

The long tail feathers are spread out to keep the bird steady while it is hovering, looking for food

I DON'T BELIEVE IT!

Hobbies are amongst the fastest, most acrobatic fliers of all. They can dive, twist and turn, bombing towards the ground at great speeds, only opening their wings a few metres above the ground.

19 Kestrels hover and look as if they are hardly moving. They fly facing the wind, staying in the same spot above the ground. Kestrels spread their tails and the feathers at their wing tips turn up, which helps them to stay steady. As they lower their heads, they get a good view of the ground and any small animals, before launching an attack.

20 Birds of prey with long, broad wings soar through the sky. They also have large, fan-shaped tails that, with their wings, catch the air like a parachute. Soaring birds, such as eagles and vultures, often wait until the air is warm before they fly. As air is heated by the Sun it rises. Large, soaring birds use these flows of warm air, called thermal uplifts, to get airborne and rise high above the ground.

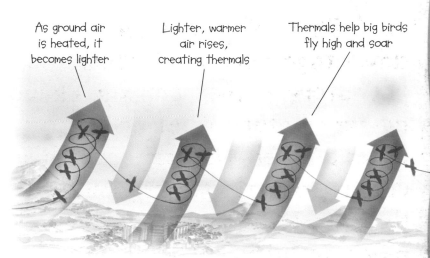

As ground air is heated, it becomes lighter

Lighter, warmer air rises, creating thermals

Thermals help big birds fly high and soar

▲ Thermals are hot air currents that travel upwards. Birds of prey use them to reach greater heights.

21 At breeding time, male birds of prey often perform display flights. These might help to attract females or mark out territory. There are different patterns of display flights, from circling round and round, to dive bombing or swooping up and down.

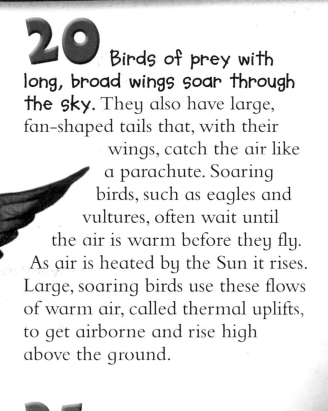

▶ At mating time, one golden eagle dives towards its mate, which turns its back, and they wrestle one another with their feet.

Nests, eggs and chicks

22 Like all birds, raptors lay eggs, usually in nests. Females may build nests in trees or on cliffs. Some birds of prey use the same nest every year, adding more sticks until it is huge. Golden eagle nests can eventually grow to 6 metres deep and 2 metres wide!

▶ Ospreys often use the same nest, year after year, so their nest becomes massive.

23 Big birds of prey have few natural predators, so only lay one or two eggs a year. Caring for chicks is hard work because they need a lot of food. If large birds of prey had more chicks, they might not be able to find enough food to feed them all and some would die. Smaller birds of prey usually breed earlier in the year and lay more eggs.

24 One egg is laid at a time and the female sits on it to keep it warm. It can take several days before all the eggs are laid. While the female protects the eggs and chicks, the male does most of the hunting and brings food to the nest. When the chicks hatch, they are covered in soft feathers called down.

▼ A peregrine falcon chick hatches from its egg.

▶ At two days old, the chick is fluffy and cheeps for food.

25 If food is scarce, the smallest chicks are not fed and die. Eagle chicks battle with each other and a larger, hungrier chick may push its brother or sister out of the nest or even eat it. It takes just a few weeks for the chicks of a small bird of prey, such as a merlin, to grow adult feathers and be able to fly, but it can take over four months for vulture chicks to reach this stage.

26 Young birds of prey may stay in their parents' care for many months. They have to learn how to hunt before they become independent, and might rely on their parents to bring them food for a whole year after hatching. When they are old enough to mate they may find a partner and stay with them for life.

▼ When it is 28 days old, the young bird is growing its adult plumage (feathers) and the old down is falling out.

▶ Juvenile peregrines have brown feathers. The face markings are paler than in older birds.

Home and away

27 **Birds of prey may fly long distances (migrate) in search of food or places to breed.** Raptors that live near the Equator don't usually migrate as their tropical homes contain enough food and are warm all year round.

▼ Migrating birds of prey follow certain routes every year. Some of the major migration routes are shown here.

Hawk Mountain

Veracruz

28 **Animals of the north struggle to survive in the cold.** Many small animals hibernate (sleep) during winter. This leaves some birds of prey hungry, so they travel south to warmer areas. Golden eagles, gyrfalcons and goshawks stay in their northerly homes unless they live in the extreme north.

▼ Every year, people gather to watch birds fly overhead at Hawk Mountain, USA.

29 **Migrating birds usually fly over land, not water.** Warm air currents that help large birds to soar for long distances develop above continents rather than oceans, so the routes avoid stretches of water. Big groups of birds may fly together over strips of land and crossing points, such as at Gibraltar, where Europe meets Africa, or the Black Sea coast.

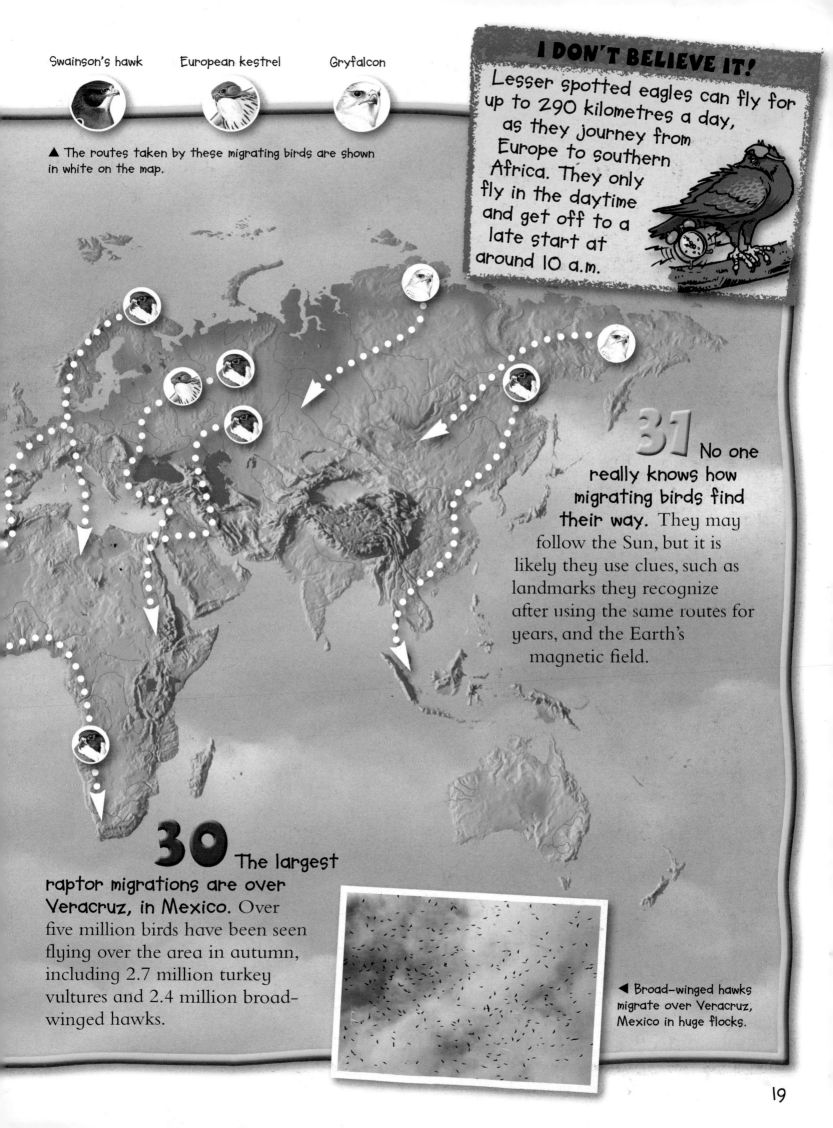

Swainson's hawk

European kestrel

Gryfalcon

▲ The routes taken by these migrating birds are shown in white on the map.

31 No one really knows how migrating birds find their way. They may follow the Sun, but it is likely they use clues, such as landmarks they recognize after using the same routes for years, and the Earth's magnetic field.

30 The largest raptor migrations are over Veracruz, in Mexico. Over five million birds have been seen flying over the area in autumn, including 2.7 million turkey vultures and 2.4 million broad-winged hawks.

◄ Broad-winged hawks migrate over Veracruz, Mexico in huge flocks.

19

Hunting weapons

32 Predators need good senses to find prey, speed to catch it and weapons for killing it. Raptors are equipped with bodies that are ideal for locating and killing, but learning the skills to hunt takes time, patience and practice.

◄ Tawny owls have soft feathers that muffle noise, so they can take off in silence.

33 The most important weapons are feet and mouths. Raptors' bills are usually hooked, with a pointed tip. Birds that hunt other birds, such as falcons, hawks and owls, often have short, hooked bills. Those raptors that hunt larger animals need long, strong bills.

▼ This golden eagle's toes have dagger-like claws (talons) that can pierce flesh with ease.

34 Raptors' feet have talons and they are highly developed for hunting. Each foot has three strong, scaly toes at the front and one at the side or back. When the toes are bent they can grasp like a hand – perfect for holding wriggling prey.

Sharp hooks on an osprey's foot help it to grab and hold slippery fish

When a barn owl grabs its prey, its foot can spread wide to get a good gri...

...ure does not ...ry sharp talons, as it usually feeds on carrion

▲ The shape of a bird's talons depends on how it hunts and its type of prey.

35 **Feet give clues about how a bird hunts.** Birds of prey with short legs and short feet usually kill on the ground. Birds with long legs, long feet and slender, sharp talons catch and kill their prey in the air. Birds with especially big hind toes grab hold of large animals, such as rabbits or even deer.

▶ Rapid wingbeats can change the owl's direction easily.

36 **Tawny owls mostly hunt at night.** They wait on a perch, looking and listening for small animals that may be moving around nearby. They sometimes beat their wings to startle other perching birds, forcing them into flight. Once the birds are in the air, the owls can follow their movements and prepare to attack. They can even pick birds or bats off their perches or out of nests.

▶ As they prepare to grab their prey, tawny owls spread their wings to cover it and they kill it instantly with their bill and feet.

◀ Vultures and marabou storks feast on the carcass of a dead animal.

37 **Not all birds of prey hunt live prey.** Some eat any meat they can find and are called scavengers, or carrion-eaters. Some birds of prey only scavenge when they cannot find live prey, but others never hunt and only eat leftovers.

38 **Vultures are birds of prey that mostly scavenge dead animals.** They often have bald heads and necks because feathers would get messy and bloody from delving into dead bodies. Vultures often look for hyenas or lions tucking into a meal, then swoop down to feed when the coast is clear.

King vulture

Lammergeier

Lappet-faced vulture

▶ Adult griffon vultures have white feathers on their necks, a yellow-white bill and yellow-brown eyes. Youngsters have darker feathers, brown bills and eyes.

39 Griffon vultures like to wash in water after feeding. They have bare heads and necks for reaching into carcasses. These birds soar over open areas, using their long, broad wings, looking for carrion. Griffon vultures fly in groups of up to 40 for hours at a time and they may frighten other predators away to get at food.

41 African vultures take turns to munch through a body. Lappet-faced vultures have big bills that are perfect for ripping through skin and fur, so they often eat first. Hooded vultures come along later to eat softer meat, and lammergeiers (bearded vultures) tackle the leftovers.

◀ Few animals are clever enough to use tools, but Egyptian vultures can break tough eggs with stones.

40 Vultures and other scavenging birds make the most of any dining opportunities. Turkey vultures are often seen flying or perched near roads – ready to tuck in when animals and cars collide on the highway. Egyptian vultures find it difficult to break open eggs with their bill, so they use stones to crack them open instead.

◀ Vultures usually have long, thin necks that help them probe deep into a carcass to feed. Their bills are particularly long and strong, because carrion is tough to eat.

Fussy eaters

42 **Some birds of prey have unusual diets.** Lesser spotted eagles that live around wetlands feast on frogs. Snail kites have curved, hooked bills for extracting snails from their shells. Palm-nut vultures eat the fruits of palm trees.

▲ When ospreys plunge into water, they close their nostrils so the water doesn't shoot up into their nose. They carry their catch back to the nest to eat in peace or feed it to their chicks.

▶ Snail kites live in South American wetlands and eat water snails, turtles and crabs. They also hunt rodents, such as rats and mice.

43 **Plucking a fish out of water takes huge skill.** Yet some birds of prey can achieve this incredible feat. They soar over water, watching for movement at the surface. Once they have spied a fish, the birds dive down and plunge their feet into the water to grab it. This requires sharp eyesight, quick reactions and an agile body.

44 **Ospreys are fish-eaters.** These birds of prey nest near lakes and rivers or by clean, calm coastal areas. They hover up to 30 metres above the water until they spot a fish. Then they dive down with half-closed wings and stretch out their legs and feet just before hitting the water.

45 White-tailed eagles pluck both fish and ducks out of the water. They perch on trees and swoop down to grab prey. Sharp growths, called spicules, on the feet help to grip wet prey and large bills are ideal for ripping and tearing flesh.

46 Lammergeiers eat a diet of bones and scraps left behind by other predators. They pick up large bones with their feet and fly to a height of 80 metres before dropping the bones to the ground to split them. These birds also drop tortoises to get to the soft flesh inside the shell.

FISH EATERS

Penguins are flightless birds that catch fish to eat. Find out where they live and how they catch fish. How are their bodies different to those of birds of prey?

▶ If a bone is dropped from a great height it splits open. The lammergeier can then eat the soft marrow inside.

Snake stampers

Black flight feathers

Black crest feathers

47 Secretary birds are not like other raptors. They are tall, elegant and long-legged. These birds stride through the long grasses of African plains, looking for insects and other animals to eat. When they find their prey, they stamp and peck it to death.

Grey plumage on body

48 Secretary birds eat snakes, even poisonous ones, such as cobras and adders. When it spies a snake in the vegetation, a secretary bird runs towards it and stamps on it, or inflicts a kick to the head. A sharp peck to the back of the snake's neck finishes it off. If the prey proves too tough to kill this way, the bird may grab it in its beak, take to the skies and drop it from a great height.

Large feet

Long legs

▶ A male secretary bird can grow to about 1.4 metres tall. Secretary birds might get their name from the crest of long, black quill feathers on their heads, which look like old-fashioned ink pens.

QUIZ
1. How tall can a male secretary bird grow to be?
2. What are secretary birds' legs covered in?
3. How many snakes does a family of short-toed eagles need every day?

Answers:
1. About 1.4 metres 2. Thick scales 3. At least five

49 Snakes are no match for a secretary bird. These predators run fast during a chase and their legs are covered in thick scales to protect them from bites. If a snake fights back, the secretary bird spreads its wings to form a shield. The flapping wings scare the snake and if it bites a feather, the bird will suffer no harm. They often hunt in pairs and can walk more than 25 kilometres every day in search of food.

50 When they are angry, excited or scared, secretary birds raise their quill feathers. Their body feathers are grey and white, but black feathers at the top of their long legs make them appear as if they are wearing short trousers! Males and females look similar, but females are smaller.

▶ Short-toed eagles feed dead snakes to their young, which have enormous appetites.

51 Not many birds of prey eat snakes, but short-toed eagles eat almost nothing else. They attack snakes that are nearly 2 metres long and even eat poisonous ones. A family of short-toed eagles needs at least five snakes every day, so the adults spend a lot of time hunting their slithery prey.

Eagles

52 Eagles are large, heavy-bodied birds with strong legs, big bills and feet, and broad wings. They are usually smaller than vultures, but larger than most other birds of prey. There are about 60 types, including fish eagles, snake eagles, harpy eagles and hawk eagles.

53 These birds live in all regions of the world except Antarctica. Golden eagles are one of the most common, widespread types. There may be as many as one million and they live in North America, Europe and Asia, around mountains, forests and cliffs. The Great Nicobar serpent eagle is a rare eagle. It lives on one small island near India, and there may be fewer than 1000.

54 Eagles are not as agile as some other birds of prey. When they hunt, they are more likely to soar and stoop than to hover and dive. Eagles often perch to watch for prey, then swoop in low for the kill.

▼ Large birds of prey, such as eagles, rely on thermals to reach height in the sky.

2 An eagle uses thermals to reach a good height for spotting its prey, and then swoops.

1 Warm air thermals travel upwards.

4 The eagle flies off with its prey held firmly in its feet.

3 As the bird flies towards its prey, it swings its feet forward to grab hold of it.

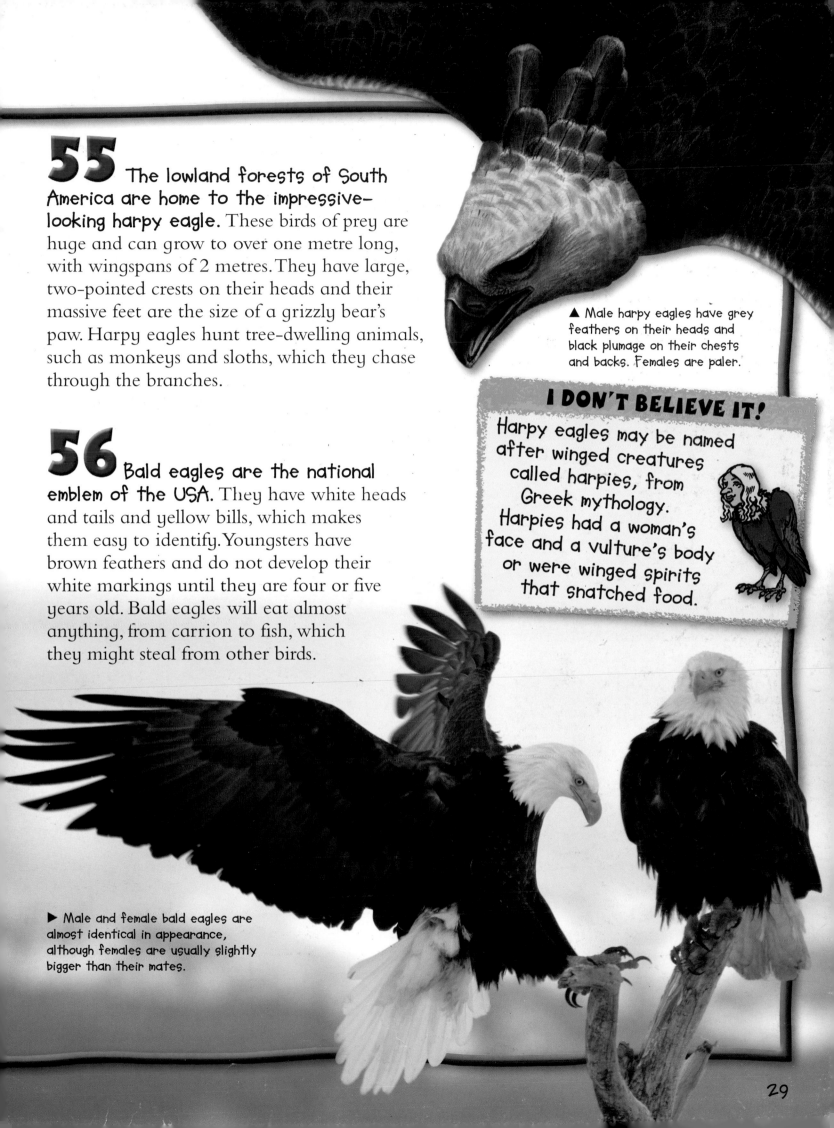

55 The lowland forests of South America are home to the impressive-looking harpy eagle. These birds of prey are huge and can grow to over one metre long, with wingspans of 2 metres. They have large, two-pointed crests on their heads and their massive feet are the size of a grizzly bear's paw. Harpy eagles hunt tree-dwelling animals, such as monkeys and sloths, which they chase through the branches.

▲ Male harpy eagles have grey feathers on their heads and black plumage on their chests and backs. Females are paler.

56 Bald eagles are the national emblem of the USA. They have white heads and tails and yellow bills, which makes them easy to identify. Youngsters have brown feathers and do not develop their white markings until they are four or five years old. Bald eagles will eat almost anything, from carrion to fish, which they might steal from other birds.

I DON'T BELIEVE IT!

Harpy eagles may be named after winged creatures called harpies, from Greek mythology. Harpies had a woman's face and a vulture's body or were winged spirits that snatched food.

▶ Male and female bald eagles are almost identical in appearance, although females are usually slightly bigger than their mates.

Kites and buzzards

57 Kites are small raptors with short bills and long, narrow wings and tails. They are elegant fliers that flap their wings slowly. Kites catch small prey, such as insects and rodents. They live throughout the world, mostly in warm places.

◀ Swallow-tailed kites rarely flap their wings while flying, but twist their tails to change direction quickly.

58 Black kites are omnivores, which means they will eat almost anything. They even scavenge rubbish. These birds live in Africa, Australia, Europe and parts of Asia, especially in woods, near farmland and water, or where humans are found. Red kites are rarer and only found in parts of Europe. They mostly eat other birds, but will also eat whatever is available.

▶ Red kites hunt over grasslands, lakes and rubbish dumps. They also search roads for roadkill.

59 Swallow-tailed kites live in tropical rainforests of South America. They have long, elegant wings and forked tails that give them the appearance of swallows. These birds can swoop, soar and dive, changing direction rapidly to pursue prey. They build their nests at the tops of tall trees.

60 Buzzards are big-bodied birds with broad wings and large, rounded tails. When they fly, they beat their wings slowly and gracefully. They eat small mammals and insects. Honey buzzards eat wasps and bees. They rip open hives with their talons and bills, then eat the larvae, pupae and adult insects. These birds have slit-like nostrils and bristles instead of feathers between their eyes, which may protect them from stings.

61 In the Americas, buzzards are often called hawks. Swainson's hawk spends summer in the USA and travels to South America for winter. When breeding, they eat mice, squirrels and reptiles, but for the rest of the year they survive mostly on insects, such as grasshoppers and beetles. They often walk along the ground looking for food and sometimes hunt in teams.

◀ A common buzzard feeds during winter. There are nearly 30 species (types) of buzzards and they belong to a group of raptors called Buteos.

QUIZ

1. Which kites have the appearance of swallows?
2. Which buzzards eat wasps and bees?
3. Which hawk sometimes hunts in teams?

Answers:
1. Swallow-tailed kites
2. Honey buzzards
3. Swainson's hawk

Fast falcons

▶ A peregrine falcon pursues a swallow. It has recently been discovered that peregrines that live in towns are able to hunt at night, helped by city lights to find their prey.

63 Peregrines are travellers and have one of the longest migrations of any raptors. American peregrines have been known to cover 25,000 kilometres in just one year. These raptors are the most widespread of all birds of prey and live on every continent except Antarctica, but they are rare.

62 A peregrine falcon can move faster than any other animal on Earth. These birds reach speeds of 100 kilometres an hour when chasing prey. When peregrines stoop from heights of one kilometre and plummet through the sky, they may reach speeds of 300 kilometres an hour or more.

▼ Saker falcons have bold markings while some Eleonora's falcons have rusty pink breast feathers.

Eleonora's falcon

Saker falcon

64 There are about 35 species of falcon and most of them are speedy fliers. They are medium-sized raptors with muscle-packed bodies, pointed wings and short tails. They usually nest in cliffs and lay several eggs at a time. Falcons prey upon birds and other small animals.

I DON'T BELIEVE IT!

At breeding time, female gyrfalcons often store food near the nest. They are able to break off frozen bits of food with their bills.

► Gyrfalcons are bulky birds with extra body fat that helps them to keep warm.

65 Gyrfalcons can cope with the cold and they live around the Earth's frozen north. Some gyrfalcons are brown or grey. The further north they live, the paler they become, so they are camouflaged against the snowy landscape. These are the biggest falcons, with a wingspan of up to 1.3 metres, so they can pursue large prey such as ptarmigans, gulls and geese.

▼ Lesser kestrels spend the winters in Africa, travelling into Europe for the summer. They mostly feed on insects, but in spring they hunt reptiles and small mammals.

66 Kestrels are types of falcon that hover before attacking their prey. These small birds of prey have rounded heads and large eyes. While male and female raptors often have the same colour plumage, male kestrels are usually more colourful than the females.

▼ Goshawks live in forested areas of Europe. They mainly hunt birds that are weak or ill because sick animals make easier targets.

67 Hawks, sparrowhawks and goshawks belong to a group of raptors called Accipiters. They are medium-sized birds and live in forests and woodlands. Short, rounded wings and long tails help them to fly in short bursts between trees, darting through branches in pursuit of small mammals and birds.

68 Most hawks hunt rodents, such as rats. They are useful because they eat pests that damage crops. However goshawks hunt game birds and poultry. Game birds, such as pheasants, are bred by farmers to be hunted for sport. Poultry, such as chickens, are an important food for humans. Goshawks have been killed to stop them from hunting these birds.

I DON'T BELIEVE IT!

Sharp–shinned hawks of America take their prey to a special perch called a butcher's block. This is where the raptor plucks all the feathers or fur off its prey, so these bits don't mess up its nest!

69 **Hawks may squeeze their prey to death.** Many raptors use their feet to hold prey and their bills to kill it. Cooper's hawks hold a captured animal with their sharp talons and fly with it until it dies. They have been known to hold prey underwater to drown it.

70 **Harriers are raptors that look similar to hawks, with long legs and tails.** They often fly low over fields and meadows, scouring the ground for snakes, frogs, insects, small birds or mammals. Hen harriers live in Europe, Asia and North America, but the populations of birds on each side of the Atlantic are slightly different from one another. North American birds are usually called marsh harriers or northern harriers.

Common black hawks live near water in Central America

▶ Hawks have rounded heads with short bills. Their compact bodies help them to fly fast and change direction.

Red-tailed hawks of North America inhabit woods, deserts and mountains

71 **Eurasian sparrowhawks are one of the most common raptors in the world.** They live in forests, farms, woods and parks across Europe and Asia during the spring and summer, and travel south for the winter. Despite being common, sparrowhawks are so secretive that they are rarely seen. However when food is scarce they may investigate gardens, searching for song birds such as sparrows to eat.

Eurasian sparrowhawks hide their nests in woodlands

72 **Most owls hunt at night.** As well as having talons and sharp bills, owls have big eyes that face the front and can see depth and movement. Eyes have two types of cells – one detecting colours, the other just faint or dim light. Some owls only have light-detecting cells and can see in the darkness, but not colour.

I DON'T BELIEVE IT!

Eurasian eagle owls have been known to kill birds as large as herons and roe deer. They have even attacked people walking their dogs near a nest.

73 **Owls use feathers to help them hear and to stop animals from hearing them.** Their ears are covered by feathers that direct sound into the ear canal. Downy feathers on the body and feet help to soften sound as the bird moves. Feathers on the wings are arranged in a way that deadens the sound of flapping, so the bird descends silently on its prey.

▲ Like some other owls, this great horned owl is nocturnal, which means that it is most active at night. It begins hunting at dusk and settles down to sleep when the Sun rises.

◄ Owls have three eyelids. The third eyelid is a special membrane that sweeps over the eye to clean it.

▶ Pellets can be opened and their contents studied to discover the diet of a bird of prey.

Pellet from a little owl

Pellet from a long-eared owl

Pellet from a barn owl

Pellet from a red kite

76 Owls eat a range of food, including insects, birds, bats and fish, and they often swallow an animal whole. Like other birds of prey, owls are not able to digest the hard parts of a body, such as bones, fur or feathers. They bring them up from their stomach and spit them out in the form of pellets. It takes about seven hours for one pellet to form.

74 Eurasian eagle owls have a wingspan of nearly 2 metres. The largest owls, they attack other birds to steal their territories. Tiny elf owls catch their prey in flight. They are the smallest owls, with a wingspan of just 15 centimetres.

75 Many birds of prey build their own nests, but owls do not. They either use old nests left by other birds, or they lay their eggs in a hole in a tree, a hollow in the ground or inside an abandoned building. Owls usually lay a clutch of up to seven eggs at a time and the chicks are called owlets.

▶ Tawny owls nest in tree hollows. They lay 2–6 eggs and the fluffy chicks do not leave the nest until they are about 35 days old.

Working birds

77 Birds of prey can be trained to work with people. This is called falconry or hawking, and is an old skill that has been around for about 2500 years. The first trained birds of prey were probably used to catch birds for people to eat. In some places it is against the law to catch wild birds for use in falconry, so birds are specially bred.

The bird may be tied to a leash

Traditional hoods are handmade from 1–3 pieces of leather that are moulded and stitched

Bells may be attached to anklets on the bird's legs or fitted to the tail

A falconer pulls the hood off using the top knot

▼ ▶ Falconers use a range of equipment to train and fly their birds, such as this peregrine falcon.

A swing lure is used to train a falcon and is made from the wing of another bird

Hood braces are gently pulled to tighten the hood on the bird's head

78 Birds most commonly trained are Harris hawks, peregrine falcons, sparrowhawks and goshawks, because they are intelligent. Training takes time and patience. The first step is to get the bird used to people. Next, it has to be trained to hop onto the falconer's gloved fist, then to fly away – and return. To start, the bird may be tied to a line, but as it learns to return, it is released. When the bird does what the falconer wants, it is rewarded with food.

79 Working raptors have been used to keep public places clear of pigeons. Pigeon poo can cause damage to buildings and spread diseases, so falconers and their birds visit city centres to stop the pigeons from nesting nearby. One sight of a swooping, soaring raptor scares the pigeons into flying elsewhere.

SEE THEM FLY
Visit a place where birds of prey are kept, so you can watch them fly. This could be a nature reserve, wildlife park or a place where trained birds of prey display their skills.

80 Birds of prey help farmers to control pests. Fields of berry-producing plants attract birds such as starlings. A flock can quickly strip the trees or bushes, leaving the farmer with no crop. Rather than covering the plants with expensive netting or spraying with chemicals, farmers ask falconers and their raptors to scare the smaller birds away.

81 Falcons can patrol airports to keep flocks of birds away from planes. If birds fly into a plane's engines, they can cause damage that is expensive to repair and can be dangerous. Airports sometimes play bird of prey calls to scare away flocks.

▶ Falcons have proved effective at keeping the skies clear of smaller birds at airports.

Bird tales

82 Throughout history, people have recognized the might and power of birds of prey and told stories about them. Native American legends tell of thunderbirds, which are large birds that create storms by flapping their wings. They also tell of an evil creature called Eagleman, which had the head of a man but the body and wings of an eagle.

▲ Native American wood carvings often showed thunderbirds with their huge bills and eyes.

▲ This ancient Greek coin is decorated with an owl.

83 Unlucky Prometheus was a character in Greek mythology. He stole fire from Zeus, the father of the gods, and gave it to mankind. This angered Zeus so much that he chained Prometheus to a rock and ordered that an eagle would eat his liver every day. By night, his liver grew back so Prometheus was destined to an eternity of pain and misery.

84 In ancient Egypt, Horus was a falcon god, worshipped as the god of the sky. According to legend, Horus's right eye was the sun and his left eye was the moon and, as he flew across the sky, the sun and moon moved with him. More than 2000 years ago, Horus' worshippers built the huge Temple of Edfu to honour him and it still stands in Egypt today, along the banks of the river Nile.

◀ Pictures of the falcon god Horus cover walls of ancient Egyptian temples and shrines.

85 **A story from Finland tells how an eagle created the Earth and the heavens.** A woman called Luonnotar was floating in a giant ocean when an eagle made a nest on her knee and laid its eggs. However the nest fell, breaking the eggs. The shells became the heavens and Earth, the yolks became the sun and the egg whites became the moon.

▶ Griffins represented godly power and were often used to guard treasure, or to protect from evil.

86 **Griffins have featured in mythology and legends from Asia to Europe.** These fabled creatures were usually shown as lions with the heads of birds of prey, especially eagles.

Watching and tracking

87 Birdwatchers are called birders, while people who study birds more scientifically are called ornithologists. They use hides to watch raptors without disturbing them. Hides are covered in natural materials, such as branches or grass, for camouflage.

▲ A bird is trapped using a hawk mist net. Data taken from the bird will help to follow its movements and how it has grown.

88 Observing birds of prey is a fascinating hobby, but it is also an important job for scientists. They collect information to learn about how the birds live, where they migrate to and how many breeding adults there are. This work can then be used to follow how populations of birds of prey in different places increase or decrease.

89 Some birds of prey are studied using leg rings and by tracking their movements. They may be captured using a mist net, which catches birds in flight without harming them. Information is collected about each bird, such as its age, sex and size before an identity ring is put around its leg, or a tag is attached to its wing.

▼ Birds like these red kites can be studied from a hide. Birders use binoculars and telescopes to zoom in and watch them closely, without disturbing them.

ORDER FALCONIFORMES

Family	Number of species or types	Examples
Accipitridae	236	Kites, hawks, goshawks, buzzards, harriers, eagles, Old World vultures, sparrowhawks
Falconidae	64	Falcons, falconets, merlins, caracaras, kestrels
Cathartidae	7	New World vultures
Pandionidae	1	Osprey
Sagittariidae	1	Secretary bird

ORDER STRIGIFORMES

Family	Number of species or types	Examples
Tytonidae	21	Barn owls, bay owls and grass owls
Strigidae	159	Burrowing owl, eagle owl, fish owl, horned owls, long-eared owl, snowy owl, hawk owl

90 **Identifying birds of prey can be difficult.** Birders look for clues to help them work out what type of raptor they are observing, such as wing, tail and head shape. Colours and banding on plumage can also be used to discover what sex a bird is and whether it is a young bird or an adult. The way a raptor flies can also provide clues to identifying it.

▲ Owls are placed in the order Strigiformes. All other raptors are in a separate order, called Falconiformes.

MAKE A NOTE

When you see any bird you do not recognize make a note of its size, the shape of its wings and tail, the way it is behaving and the type of habitat you've seen it in. Use this information to discover its identity from a birdwatching book or website.

Raptors in peril

91 Birds of prey face few natural dangers, except those posed by humans and their way of life. Around half of all the world's species of migrating raptors are threatened with extinction. Many of these may die out because they are hunted or because their habitats are destroyed or polluted.

92 Raptors are killed by people who believe they are pests. Poison can be added to their food and left out for them to eat, or they may be shot. Birds and eggs are sometimes stolen from the wild by collectors or people who want to train birds for hawking or falconry.

▼ At night, barn owls may be confused by lights on roads or near towns and fly into the path of oncoming vehicles. Raptors can also be pulled into the sides of fast-moving lorries or cars.

Normal egg   Poisoned egg

▲ When female birds eat poisoned food, the poisons travel through their bodies and may reach the eggs growing inside them.

93
Habitats are damaged by chemicals used in farming or waste products from factories. When these chemicals enter birds' bodies – often by eating prey that have already been affected by them – they may cause permanent damage. Some chemicals stop eggshells from growing properly, so birds cannot produce healthy chicks.

▶ Long-billed vultures, such as this juvenile, are endangered.

94
When birds of prey drop in number, the environment suffers. Three species of Asian vultures help to stop the spread of disease to humans and other animals by eating carrion, but millions of these birds have died in just over ten years. The vultures are dying because a drug that is used to treat farm animals is deadly to any raptors that feed on their bodies.

95
Bateleurs live in open country across Africa, but their numbers are falling fast. They are struggling to survive because their natural habitat is being turned into farmland. Some large farming organizations are also poisoning them on purpose.

▶ Bateleur nests are disturbed as people settle near their habitats. Many birds are also trapped to be sold abroad.

Rescuing raptors

96 The Philippine eagle is one of the rarest raptors, but people are working hard to save it. There are probably fewer than 250 breeding pairs in the wild, although scientists have managed to breed them in captivity. The largest of all eagles, these birds have lost their homes to farmland and mines. Now they are protected by law and their land, nests and eggs are guarded.

▲ Even if the numbers of Philippine eagles stop falling, it may be impossible for the species to recover in the wild.

▶ Californian condors died in huge numbers after eating animals that had been shot with lead bullets. Lead is a poison that is still found in the environment.

97 People who are interested in birds work together to protect them. BirdLife International is an organization that operates in more than 100 countries. It helps local conservation agencies protect birds' habitats and teach people how to respect the environment.

98 Californian condors are vultures with wingspans of nearly 3 metres. They do not breed until they are about nine years old and only have one chick every two years. These birds once lived all over the USA, but by the 1980s there were very few left. They were all taken into captivity, making a total of 22. Since then they have been bred in protected places and some have been returned to the wild.

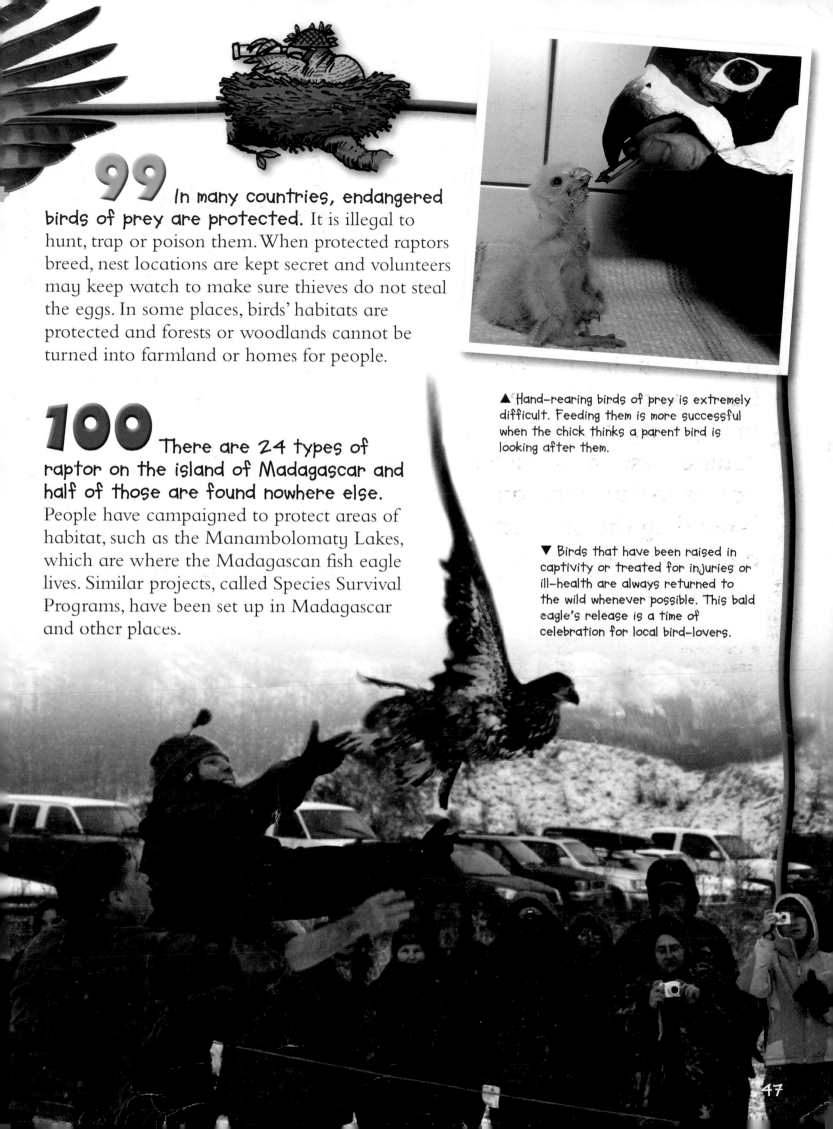

99 In many countries, endangered birds of prey are protected. It is illegal to hunt, trap or poison them. When protected raptors breed, nest locations are kept secret and volunteers may keep watch to make sure thieves do not steal the eggs. In some places, birds' habitats are protected and forests or woodlands cannot be turned into farmland or homes for people.

100 There are 24 types of raptor on the island of Madagascar and half of those are found nowhere else. People have campaigned to protect areas of habitat, such as the Manambolomaty Lakes, which are where the Madagascan fish eagle lives. Similar projects, called Species Survival Programs, have been set up in Madagascar and other places.

▲ Hand-rearing birds of prey is extremely difficult. Feeding them is more successful when the chick thinks a parent bird is looking after them.

▼ Birds that have been raised in captivity or treated for injuries or ill-health are always returned to the wild whenever possible. This bald eagle's release is a time of celebration for local bird-lovers.

Index